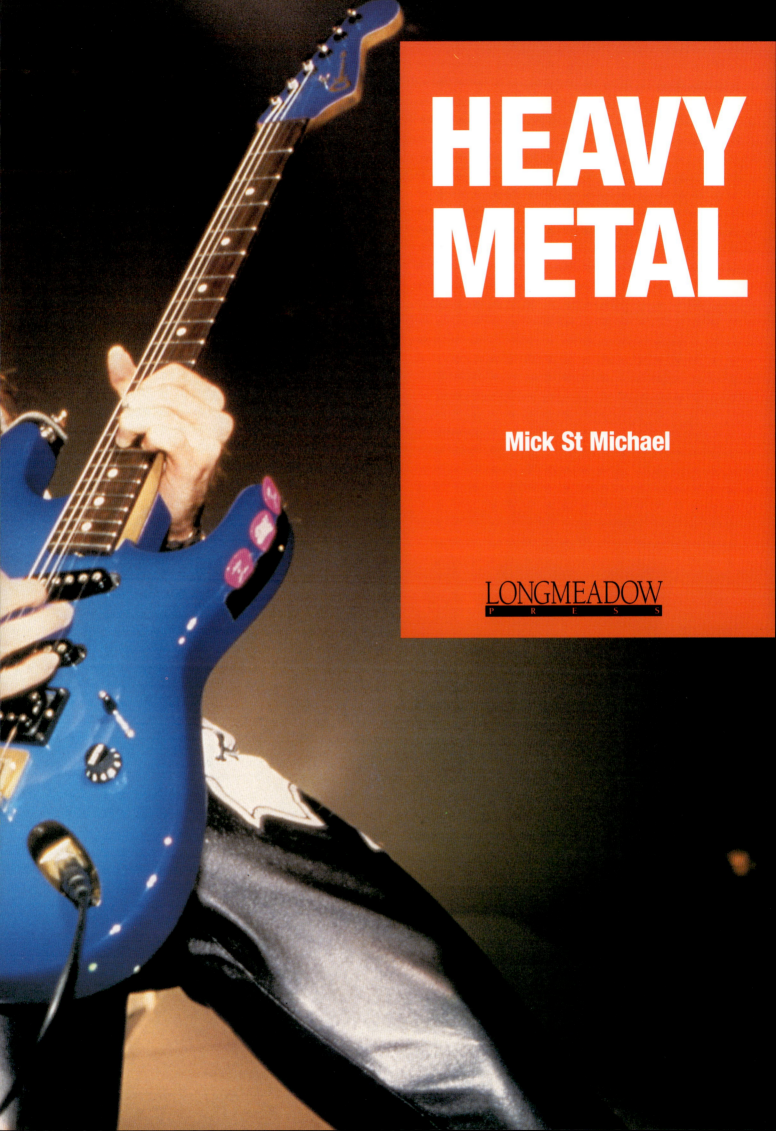

HEAVY METAL

Mick St Michael

LONGMEADOW PRESS

THE ROOTS OF METAL	6
THE SEVENTIES SUPERGROUPS	14
THE EIGHTIES NEW WAVE	30
THE FUTURE	46
INDEX	64

Copyright © 1992 Brompton Books Corporation

All rights reserved. No part of this publication may be reproduced, stored in a retrieval system or transmitted in any form by any means, electronic, mechanical, photocopying or otherwise, without first obtaining the written permission of the copyright owner.

This 1992 edition published by
Longmeadow Press
201 High Ridge Road
Stamford CT 06904

Produced by
Brompton Books Corporation
15 Sherwood Place
Greenwich CT 06830

ISBN 0-681-41678-5

Printed in Hong Kong

0987654321

PAGE 1 1989 US chart-toppers Poison (from left) Rikki Rockett, Bobby Dall (background), Bret Michaels and CC Deville.

PAGES 2-3 Ozzy Osbourne takes a bite out of guitarist Zakk Wilde. He proved as successful in his solo career as he had been in Black Sabbath.

PAGE 4 Guitarist Adrian Vandenberg, who led his own self-named band before linking with David Coverdale in Whitesnake.

LEFT Axl Rose, the All-American boy fronting Guns N' Roses, the self-styled 'Most Dangerous Band In The World', and heavy metal's top box-office draw in the 1990s.

THE ROOTS OF METAL

THE ROOTS OF METAL

'If heavy metal didn't exist, someone would have had to invent it.' So said one eminent critic about the musical genre that inspires fanatical loyalty and never, *ever* goes out of fashion. Visit any industrial town from Pittsburgh to Poland and you'll find the fans in denim and leather, bedecked with patches, badges and sometimes even tattoos clearly indicating their tribal loyalties.

The musical roots of heavy metal lie in psychedelia. As the Summer of Love ran out of steam, and the 1960s ended with a jolt at Altamont, music was gearing up for a new decade and wondering which direction to take. Guitar heroes were all the rage, and chief among them were Eric Clapton and Jimi Hendrix.

Clapton had come up through the ranks of the Yardbirds, a blues-based band which proved a rich breeding ground for six-string stars: his replacements were Jeff Beck and, later, Jimmy Page. Cream, the first of rock's power trios formed in 1966, became renowned for their improvisation and volume: with room to stretch out, all three of the band's instrumental virtuosi – Clapton, bassist Jack Bruce and drummer Ginger Baker – could indulge themselves in displays of instrumental pyrotechnics the like of which had never been seen before. The live portions of their albums *Wheels Of Fire* and *Goodbye* were undeniably impressive – but one band wasn't big enough for three bandleaders, and their brief, bright career lasted only from mid-1966 to 1968. After another, less successful supergroup, Blind Faith (containing Clapton and Baker), exploded shortly after take-off, the guitarist retired to temporary anonymity. But the genre he helped create was already assuming a life of its own.

LEFT 1960s' stars the Yardbirds, with Eric Clapton at right. After a spell with John Mayall, he founded supertrio Cream.

7

THE ROOTS OF METAL

Hendrix, too, had explored the power trio idea and taken rock into new areas. His extensive use of feedback, outrageous stage showmanship and championing of the guitar as phallic symbol had many admirers. Others, like Yes's Steve Howe, would take Hendrix's inspiration in a progressive direction. But from self-confessed superfans like Frank Marino, Robin Trower and Jeff Healey to those less obviously influenced, Hendrix's legacy is immense.

Though he only released four studio albums in his lifetime (which ended in his drug-induced death in 1970), Hendrix has remained a figure of immense power and influence: in 1991, *Melody Maker* announced he was the musician most quoted as an influence in their 'musicians wanted' ads, while a *Radio 1* sessions album released in 1988 sold 100,000 copies despite being composed of known and much-bootlegged material.

In the States Vanilla Fudge had created their own little bit of history by taking the Supremes' uptempo *You Keep Me Hangin' On* and transforming it into a lumbering Top Ten leviathan. (The Fudge rhythm section later linked with Jeff Beck to form short-lived supergroup Beck, Bogert and Appice.) This was one of several inspirational single tracks from a variety of artists that pointed the way to others: Steppenwolf's leather-clad image reinforced the link between heavy metal and motorbikes. They also arguably invented the music's tag: their 1968 hit *Born To Be Wild* used the phrase 'heavy metal thunder,' derived from William Burroughs's novel *The Naked Lunch*.

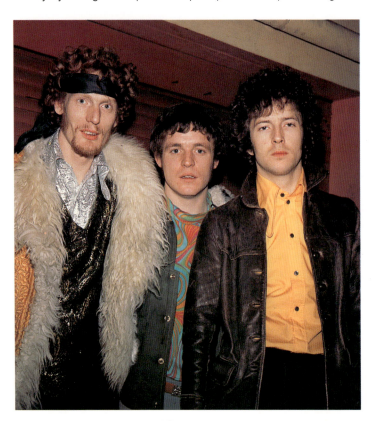

ABOVE **Ginger Baker, Jack Bruce and Eric Clapton**, collectively Cream, whose brief 1966-68 lifespan pointed to the possibilities of high-volume improvised rock and laid the foundations of metal to come.

RIGHT American proto-metal outfit Vanilla Fudge pictured at a 1980s reunion, with bassist Tim Bogert at center mike. The band's ultra-heavy sound was founded on the organ of Mark Stein and inspired Britain's Deep Purple to emulate them.

THE ROOTS OF METAL

RIGHT The unmistakable Jimi Hendrix, whose influence on rock in general and heavy metal in particular is incalculable. His death in 1970 robbed music of a uniquely innovative talent, the shockwaves from which are still audible today.

LEFT Steppenwolf, led by the be-shaded, German-born John Kay (right), turned in an early classic with 1968's *Born To Be Wild*, later covered by bands as diverse as Slade and Blue Oyster Cult.

THE ROOTS OF METAL

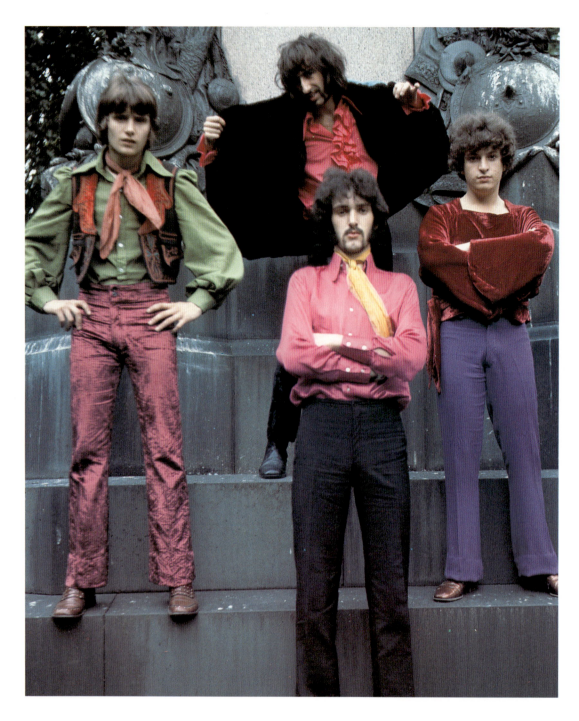

Arthur Brown's *Fire*, released on the same label as Hendrix in 1968, was a hit psychedelic/metal hybrid. Organist Vincent Crane from Brown's backing group formed Atomic Rooster, a more straightforwardly metallic trio who hit big with *Tomorrow Night* and *Devil's Answer*. Other psychedelic artists touched on metal, as in Pink Floyd's *Nile Song*. But the link between 1960s' rock and the heavy metal of the 1970s was never more evident than in the movement of the Yardbirds. Clapton's replacements Jeff Beck and Jimmy Page took the band ever further from its blues roots, establishing the guitar as the group's *raison d'être* and siring the Jeff Beck Group and Led Zeppelin in the late 1960s and early 1970s (though Beck swiftly transferred allegiance to jazz-rock).

ABOVE **The Crazy World of Arthur Brown also featured Carl Palmer (left) and Vincent Crane (center) as well as their extrovert leader (top). Their 1968 hit *Fire* straddled the worlds of psychedelia and metal.**

RIGHT **Organist Crane grew his hair and formed the ultra-heavy Atomic Rooster, one of the premier concert attractions of the early 1970s.**

THE ROOTS OF METAL

THE ROOTS OF METAL

As the heavy-metal bandwagon gathered momentum, many others leapt aboard. A Birmingham blues band called Earth took the hint and cranked up the volume, renaming themselves Black Sabbath after the title track of their first album (recorded for just over £400 in a primitive studio).

This mixture of black magic and metal proved useful in stirring up publicity and attracting inquisitive youth. Also helpful was a hit single, *Paranoid*, which reached Number 4 in Britain and encouraged interest in the States. Singer John 'Ozzy' Osbourne's high-pitched screaming contrasted boldly with Tony Iommi's powerhouse guitar riffs, with support from bassist 'Geezer' Butler and drummer Bill Ward. But personality clashes and Ozzy's alcohol problems contributed to a split between man and band, declared final in 1978 after eight UK Top Twenty albums.

Status Quo had been psychedelic two-hit wonders whose fame had failed to last. They sensed a need for music that was unpretentious and stripped back to basics. Growing their hair, losing their organist and dressing in denims, they started establishing a grass-roots support that sustained them over two successful decades. Grand Funk Railroad pursued a similar course in the States – vilified by the press, yet attracting a street following that, when the time was right, would push them and their chosen genre to the top of the charts. Slightly later on Mountain were the States' other leading practitioners; their bassist Felix Pappalardi had produced Cream and took their power trio formula to its heaviest limit with overweight guitarist Leslie West.

As the 1960s ended, kids were looking for something different – something that would see them through a decade of violence, unemployment and strife. Heavy metal was their chosen outlet – and music would never be the same again.

THE ROOTS OF METAL

FAR LEFT Black Sabbath leader Tony Iommi, who kept his band going through many personnel changes from the late 1960s to the 1990s.

LEFT The early classic Sabbath line-up (from left) Terry 'Geezer' Butler, Iommi, Bill Ward and Ozzy Osbourne.

ABOVE 'The Great Fatsby,' as Mountain axeman Leslie West self-mockingly styled himself, flashes his fingers across a rare Dan Armstrong guitar.

RIGHT Status Quo guitarist Rick Parfitt saw his band progress from psychedelic flops to denim-clad heavy-metal heroes turning out 12-bar rock *par excellence*. The band celebrated their 25th anniversary in 1990.

THE SEVENTIES SUPERGROUPS

THE SEVENTIES SUPERGROUPS

Led Zeppelin, the biggest rock band of their era, exemplified heavy metal at its most appealing. Mixing sword-and-sorcery imagery with a hint of black magic (courtesy of guitarist Jimmy Page's well publicized interest in Aleister Crowley) and a large helping of sexuality supplied by lead singer Robert 'Percy' Plant, they stood astride the heavy-metal world. Drummer John Bonham (whose drink-assisted death in 1980 ended the band's career) supplied a mighty motive power, while quiet man John Paul Jones (real name John Baldwin), who'd worked with Page on Donovan's *Hurdy Gurdy Man* single, filled in the gaps with bass and keyboards.

Zeppelin were different: instrumentally more than able and with a lingering association with hippie culture (the Orient, drugs), they attracted almost as many female as male followers – unlike the vast majority of heavy metal bands whose unprepossessing image served as a male role model.

Initially known as the New Yardbirds (but billed as such only on a Scandinavian tour which Page was contractually obliged to do), they found their name courtesy of the Who's Keith Moon, who thought their music would go down like the proverbial lead balloon in Britain. They repaid the compliment by refusing to release singles in their home country: they were a serious group and wished to be treated as such.

LEFT **Led Zeppelin re-formed for Atlantic Records' 40th birthday party in 1988, re-emphasizing the unique magic that existed between surviving members, bass player John Paul Jones (left background), guitarist Jimmy Page (center) and vocalist Robert Plant. On this occasion, Jason Bonham (son of deceased drummer John) made up the numbers.**

THE SEVENTIES SUPERGROUPS

THE SEVENTIES SUPERGROUPS

They got their wish. If *Led Zeppelin I* was a tasty *hors d'oeuvres*, their second album – which notched up advance orders of 400,000 – put the icing on the cake. Critics could say they missed the heavy-metal singles boom capitalized upon by Deep Purple and Black Sabbath – but when they refused record company pleas to put out *Whole Lotta Love* as a single, the album sold like a single itself, displacing the Beatles' *Abbey Road* at the top of the charts. Four US tours in 1969 had made them the hottest box-office property around. Their growing musical maturity was down to Plant, who had a hand in all the second album's material – having written none of the first.

1970's *Led Zeppelin III* and '71's *Four Symbols* continued the development away from *clichéd* heavy blues-based rock and into different areas like folk, though this was initially resisted by fans: the third album had enormous advance orders, but sold less well after release. They were so big that several of their albums dispensed with a group name or even record title on the cover.

Their 1970s' albums all incorporated different musical influences (the mock-reggae *D'yer Maker* on *Houses Of The Holy*, for instance), yet the band still rocked hard live – as 1976's *The Song Remains the Same* proved beyond doubt. It was accompanied by a concert film intercut with mystical sequences about the individual members. But Plant's 1975 involvement in an auto crash and the accidental death of his son understandably reduced their level of activity.

September 1980 saw the Zeppelin story draw to a close with the death of John Bonham – and though the band have sporadically re-formed for Live Aid and the Atlantic label's 40th Birthday, their comparative unwillingness to retread the past has let the legend retain its luster. Their continuing influence was underlined in 1990 when the first ever Zeppelin compilations were released and charted high.

LEFT **Zeppelin's Jimmy Page attacks his distinctive double-necked Gibson SG while John Paul Jones (background) adds keyboards. The band were exceptionally versatile for a four-piece, veering from folky melodies to fully-fledged pomp-rock in the course of one of their legendary three-hour shows that sold out auditoriums worldwide.**

ABOVE **A typically bare-chested Robert Plant in his Zeppelin prime. Plant was the only member to make a success of a solo career in the 1980s, and this seems to have ensured that a permanent re-formation of HM's biggest ever band will remain a pipedream.**

RIGHT **The Live Aid line-up backstage 1985, with supporting musicians Paul Martinez (standing left) and Tony Thompson (standing right).**

THE SEVENTIES SUPERGROUPS

Page's erstwhile lead guitar partner in the Yardbirds Jeff Beck produced two classic albums of prime heavy metal, *Truth* and *Beck-Ola* in 1968-69. Notable for Rod Stewart on vocals and future Rolling Stone Ron Wood, then on bass, they stunned the States and proved a launch-pad for Wood and Stewart to find 1970s' stardom. Beck re-formed his group with others, but moved swiftly toward jazz-rock: he'd bowed out of the Yardbirds during their ninth US tour, and was clearly not keen on life on the road – a prerequisite for any heavy band looking for a following.

Ten Years After also revolved around an axe hero, Alvin Lee, and also went down bigger in the States than in their homeland. Coming from blues roots, the Nottingham quartet made their name at Woodstock with a near 20-minute *I'm Going Home* and built a successful career around Lee's guitarwork thereafter. They split in 1975, having completed 28 marathon US tours, but re-formed after over a decade's absence in the late 1980s – their continuing success evidence that alone among the pop styles heavy metal was seldom guilty of 'ageism.'

Several rock groups operated on the periphery of metal in the 1970s such as Free, the Faces and Humble Pie, though all would have resented the tag. Yet they are worth noting as influences on such 1990s' bands as the Black Crowes and Guns N' Roses: indeed, Free's *All Right Now* – one of the great all-time rock anthems – charted in 1991 after use in a TV gum commercial.

Heavy metal has always retained an ability to shock, if only through sheer volume. Clergyman's son Vincent Furnier went further: the Detroit-born singer, who changed his name to Alice Cooper, managed to alienate a generation of parents in a short space of time – and in doing so acquired the unqualified loyalty of hundreds of thousands of kids.

Cooper's musical specialty was the rock anthem, like his early 1970s' hits *School's Out* and *Elected*. The man and his band had made an immediate impact in post-hippie Los Angeles. 'Everybody was into peace and love, and here we come looking like *A Clockwork Orange*,' he commented after an early appearance that cleared the room within just three songs. Another late-1960s' appearance saw him down the bill to John Lennon at the Toronto Peace Festival in 1969 when someone threw a chicken onstage: Cooper returned it to sender with some force, resulting in headlines like 'Alice Cooper rips chicken's head off, drinks blood.' The die was cast . . .

His stage act majored on the decapitation of plastic babies, a fascination with snakes (principally a 15-foot python) and eventually his own mock execution. Such shock-rock brought results, but proved impossible to top – and when his band defected to become the Billion Dollar Babies, Cooper/Furnier was on the slide into an alcoholic haze and musical oblivion.

But Cooper retained his credibility even when times were hard, and found that many 1990s' idols had idolized *him* way back in the 1970s. He celebrated by coming back with *Trash* in 1989 and appearing on Extreme's multi-platinum *Pornograffiti*, while his own 1991 album *Hey Stoopid* featured guest stars ranging from Ozzy Osbourne to Mötley Crüe and hot axe duo Joe Satriani and Steve Vai.

Cooper's legacy was immense: groups like Kiss and Twisted Sister took on the facepaint, while in the 1990s shock-rockers like GWAR were still taking leaves out of his rock theater manual.

THE SEVENTIES SUPERGROUPS

TOP LEFT The Jeff Beck Group's classic line-up (from left) Micky Waller (drums), Beck, Rod Stewart (vocals) and Ron Wood (bass). Their two late-1960s' albums established them as competitors for the world heavy-metal crown.

FAR LEFT Ten Years After's calling card was the fantastic fretwork skills of guitarist Alvin Lee (right), one of the speediest guitarists in rock.

ABOVE AND RIGHT Alice Cooper and friends. Notorious in the early 1970s for his stage act featuring snakes and dolls, Alice found a new audience for his greasepaint and gore dramas in the late 1980s.

THE SEVENTIES SUPERGROUPS

BELOW **Deep Purple in early action with the classic line-up (from left) Lord, Gillan, Paice, Blackmore and Glover.**

RIGHT **German supergroup Scorpions entertain a capacity audience. They ranked second only to Van Halen in the 1980s on the US stadium circuit.**

Though they initially dabbled in black-magic imagery with songs like *Devil's Eye* and *Mandrake Root*, Deep Purple went through a number of changes before emerging as one of the 1970s' hardest, heaviest and loudest groups (an entry in the *Guinness Book of Records* attested to the last boast). Revealingly they were initially planned as Britain's answer to Vanilla Fudge.

Their first bass player and singer were replaced by Roger Glover and Ian Gillan (whose pedigree included singing lead on the *Jesus Christ Superstar* rock opera LP) to create the classic line-up that recorded 1970's *In Rock*, one of the decade's most influential metal albums. As well as Gillan's past form, organist Jon Lord was classically trained – something that led to a false move in 1969's live *Concerto For Group And Orchestra*. Once on the hard-rock road, however, Purple got their teeth into the music and wouldn't let go.

Their formula of soaring vocals from Gillan and often inspired improvisation (from Lord and guitarist Ritchie Blackmore) with repetitive riffing proved a money-spinner. *In Rock* sold a million, the single *Black Night* reached Number 2 in Britain and the stage was set for a further set of three US million-sellers that duplicated their successes at home. Only when Gillan and Glover left did the rot set in, when a soul-music influence was imported via new bassist Glenn Hughes and the band split in 1976. The classic line-up re-formed some eight years later to record a series of Top Ten albums.

THE SEVENTIES SUPERGROUPS

LEFT **AC/DC's ever-youthful Angus Young in trademark schoolboy attire. His digital dexterity belied the fancy dress and helped the Australians to world stardom.**

RIGHT **Judas Priest vocalist Rob Halford is the meat in an axe sandwich between guitarists Tipton and Downing. Initial Japanese success was soon duplicated in Britain and the States.**

Australia had contributed little to the hard-rock scene before AC/DC arrived. There was, however, a link to the Easybeats, 1960s' hitmakers with *Friday On My Mind*, whose George Young and Harry Vanda produced the new band, Young's guitarist brothers Malcolm and Angus providing the musical backbone. The band's name, incidentally, owed everything to their electric stage performance and nothing to their highly conventional sexual orientation.

They had to come to England to make an international mark, starting from scratch in the London pubs. Unfashionable as punk reared its spiky head, they proved they could be every bit as outrageous as the new wave, with the diminutive Angus in schoolboy cap and shorts strafing the front rows with his Gibson. Pretty soon they'd graduated to the stadia, but in the process lost vocalist Bon Scott who died after a drinking spree in 1980. Calling their next album *Back In Black* as a token of respect, AC/DC returned with new British singer Brian Johnson whose gravelly tones slotted in alongside Young's guitar.

THE SEVENTIES SUPERGROUPS

English had always been the international language of rock, putting foreign bands at something of a disadvantage. Germany, however, could boast the American Forces' influence. By far the biggest band ever to come out of Germany, the Scorpions struggled long and hard before breaking through in the late 1970s with the transatlantic hit albums *Lovedrive, Animal Magnetism* and *Blackout*. In the meanwhile they'd spawned various spinoffs like the Michael Schenker Group and Electric Sun, founded by Schenker's successor Uli John Roth.

Like UFO, to whom Schenker had initially defected, they broke big in Germany and Japan long before they made it to the world stage – and it was Schenker's guest appearance on *Lovedrive* alongside brother Rudolf that marked the beginning of their second phase. They ranked second only to Van Halen in the US stadium circuit in the mid-1980s, retaining momentum through original members Rudolf Schenker and vocalist Klaus Meine.

The Scorpions grew through the 1980s, adding subtlety to their repertoire and hit the charts worldwide in the early 1990s with the epic *Wind Of Change* written about the collapse of the Eastern Bloc and featuring film footage from the unsuccessful 1991 anti-Gorbachev coup in its evocative video.

Some metal bands made a virtue out of near-anonymity. Initially hugely unfashionable, Wolverhampton's Judas Priest emerged from England's bleak industrialized Midlands to become a real force in metal. They announced their presence by two early-1970s albums on the small Gull label – but it was the switch to CBS (now Sony) that saw them build an international reputation. The Japanese were among the first to appreciate Priest's appeal, though they eventually broke through at home to score pop hit singles with a string of scarf-wavers like *Take On The World* and *United*, rivaling Queen in the rock-anthem genre. 'We were never ashamed to be called a heavy metal band,' insisted singer Rob Halford. 'There's no greater form of rock'n'roll.'

Their worst moment was when they were sued in the US courts by parents of two Nevada youths who claimed backwards messages in the album *Stained Class* compelled them to fulfil a suicide pact. The 1990 hearing was an important test case for musicians worldwide in their stand against censorship, and was duly thrown out of court.

Heavy metal has always been a grass-roots movement, capable of supporting bands with a reputation for their live performance even when their record sales are negligible. This often leads to an 'iceberg' of invisible support that suddenly pushes the band into view as an 'overnight' success. Uriah Heep were one such band. Emerging in late 1969 from the unsuccessful

covers band Spice, Heep based their longevity round a ruling triumvirate of guitarist Mick Box, vocalist David Byron and keyboardist Ken Hensley: other members changed frequently. With a rhythm section of Gary Thain (bass) and Lee Kerslake (drums) that remained stable from 1972-75 they cut five albums that all reached the US Top Forty: two charted in Britain, though they were far more successful elsewhere in Europe. But as Hensley related later, 'As soon as we were making money we ran into problems . . . usually concerning ego. Demanding limousines, champagne in the dressing rooms, constant star treatment and all that sort of thing.' By the end of the decade, only Box remained of the classic line-up and of the refugees both Thain and Byron had died young.

Like Heep, UFO were unsung heroes of British metal who kept the flag flying in the late 1970s when the music went through a comparatively fallow period. Led by vocalist Phil Mogg, they were initially big in Japan and Germany: their second effort, the live *UFO Landed Japan* wasn't even given British release. Mogg, Pete Way (bass) and Andy Parker (drums) went through a succession of guitarists before striking lucky fourth time out with German guitar god Michael Schenker. With his Aryan good looks and Flying V guitar, Schenker raised the profile and, signed to Chrysalis, they climbed the ladder: *Obsession* (1978) was a transatlantic Top Fifty success.

THE SEVENTIES SUPERGROUPS

But Schenker quit to rejoin the Scorpions, ultimately going solo, and the band never topped the classic 1978 concert double *Strangers In The Night*, a British Number 7 album. Though they continued into the mid-1980s and survived Way's departure, Mogg's well-documented breakdown on tour left UFO with 'No Place To Run,' to quote an album title. They did return in the late 1980s with Mogg still at the helm but unfortunately little of the appeal remained.

As Britain struggled with industrial stagnation in the 1970s, many bored youths from the provinces formed bands. Nazareth from Scotland rolled on into the 1990s from their 1969 beginnings in Dunfermline, while Wales's Budgie were similarly grass-roots in support but, unlike Nazareth, were unable to boost their appeal by producing hit singles.

Meat Loaf (real name Marvin Lee Aday) was a human phenomenon – a man-mountain who, with the help of eccentric songwriter/producer Jim Steinman, produced a musical phenomenon of equal proportions. This was *Bat Out Of Hell*, an album released in 1978 that melded metal with Wagnerian overtones.

Meat Loaf could never top his first achievement (though the follow-up album topped the UK chart), and a later estrangement from Svengali Steinman saw him lose direction completely. But in 1991 *Bat Out Of Hell* was relaunched with an extra track featuring his vocal duet with Cher, *Dead Ringer* – and its UK chart life (395 weeks by the end of 1989) resumed unabated.

OPPOSITE ABOVE **Uriah Heep's David Byron (left) and John Wetton share a vocal moment. Hard-working Heep soldiered on into the 1990s but without these two: Byron died in 1985.**

ABOVE **The aptly named Meat Loaf goes in for a rare axe attack. Released in 1978, his *Bat Out Of Hell* is one of the longest-running stories in UK chart history.**

LEFT **UFO's Pete Way and Paul Chapman in action. The band managed to push out of the second division of metal in the 1970s with frequent touring, re-forming to give stardom another shot in the 1990s.**

THE SEVENTIES SUPERGROUPS

'If it's too loud, you're too old' was Ted Nugent's maxim – a statement that applies to everything the Detroit axeman ever recorded. After playing in highschool bands, Nugent's career took off with a move to Chicago in 1965 where he formed the Amboy Dukes. In 1968, *Journey To The Center Of The Mind* was released as a single and blasted into the national charts, eventually peaking at Number 16, but none of the Dukes' albums made a major showing.

Nugent returned with a self-titled solo album which charted in America and the UK, while *Free For All* featured the then-unknown Meat Loaf on vocals. 1977 saw Nugent at the peak of popularity despite the punk-rock explosion with the platinum *Cat Scratch Fever* and self-explanatory *Double Live Gonzo*.

A decade of falling sales saw him shelve his solo career, joining forces with ex-Nightranger man Jack Blades and guitarist Tommy Shaw from Styx to form the supergroup Damn Yankees. Released in 1990, their debut album attained platinum status – Ted Nugent was back!

Kiss mixed hard rock and theater in equal proportions to create an image that remained long after the memories of the music had faded. Taking Alice Cooper's facepaint as their cue, they each adopted an individual persona, declining to be pictured without makeup to excite press attention. 'You had to have real guts to get up on stage and look weird,' admitted Gene Simmons.

THE SEVENTIES SUPERGROUPS

LEFT **Ted Nugent in solitary splendor. One of metal's most lovable characters, 'the Nug' started life as an Amboy Duke and plays on as a Nightranger after selling millions of solo records in the 1970s.**

RIGHT **Kiss founder Gene Simmons shows he can shock even without his make-up. Together with Paul Stanley, he ensured Kiss were still cranking out rock riffs long after the 1970s.**

BELOW **A typically over-the-top Kiss stage set. 1975's *Kiss Alive* made the breakthrough to chart success for the New York four-piece.**

THE SEVENTIES SUPERGROUPS

The image disguised a hard-rocking outfit. Simmons, guitarists Paul Stanley and Ace Frehley and drummer Peter Criss were workmanlike in the studio, but stunning on stage where they acted out their sexually charged rock fantasies: Simmons's fire-eating and flashbombs inspired first derision, then devotion. 1975's *Kiss Alive* did for them what *Frampton Comes Alive* did for Peter Frampton, cashing in on their heavy touring schedule and accelerating sales of their three previous albums. From then on it was gold and platinum all the way.

Kiss came clean in the 1980s, though reaction to 1980's *Unmasked* was lukewarm and led to a readoption of the facepaint 'n' firework routine. Criss was replaced by Eric Carr and Frehley by Vinnie Vincent, then Mark Norton, but the Simmons-Stanley axis held good into the 1990s. Having painted themselves into a corner with their image, Kiss had resurfaced to compete on their own terms. Yet their image, logo and carefully packaged music had been an object lesson to those who desired success from metal excess. The stronger the image, to be reproduced on patches or other memorabilia, the better.

Boston's Aerosmith enjoyed two leases of life – one drug-assisted, the second somewhat less fraught but equally

LEFT **Kiss bassist Gene Simmons attacks his instrument.**

BELOW **Randy Bachman (left) and fellow Bachman Turner Overdriver Blair Thornton.**

RIGHT **Aerosmith's Steven Tyler, one of the band's Toxic Twins with guitarist Joe Perry who came through the excess of the 1970s to impress a new generation in a new decade.**

entertaining. Like the Rolling Stones, they were based around a singer/guitarist songwriting team, Steve Tyler (ironically a Jagger lookalike) and Joe Perry – but while the Stones were the Glimmer Twins the Aerosmith duo rejoiced in the banner the Toxic Twins. 'The thinking was, who knows how long this is going to last,' admitted Perry, 'In the meantime, have fun.' That 'excess all areas' attitude saw his partner Tyler go through four rehabilitation centers before his comeback was assured.

They made waves in the 1970s when the ballad *Dream On* from their first album reached Number 6, but it was untypical of their riff-heavy rock. They emphasized their British inspirations by playing the Yardbirds' *Train Kept A-Rollin'* as a live showcase. The momentum slackened when the Tyler-Perry axis was split in 1978, but the band returned in the late 1980s, going mega-platinum in 1989 with *Pump* as bands from Bon Jovi to Guns N' Roses encouraged their fans to tune in to one of the major influences on their music.

THE SEVENTIES SUPERGROUPS

Canada's contribution to heavy-metal history rested in the hands of Bachman Turner Overdrive and Rush. BTO were built around the axe-wrestling of ex-Guess Who star Randy Bachman, while Rush – arguably as much progressive rockers in Yes style as hard rockers – mixed philosophical lyrics with massive slabs of sound created by a three-piece line-up led by bassist/vocalist Geddy Lee.

Ireland's Thin Lizzy represented the sensitive end of metal, having graduated from blues and folk-influenced rock to an altogether harder, more metallic sound and image. Their driving force was Phil Lynott, a black Irishman who played bass and sang. Before a drug-hastened demise he was responsible for a string of fine albums. The definitive Lizzy performance was captured in 1978 on *Live And Dangerous*, an album which reached Number 2 in Britain and showed off the twin-guitar attack of Brian Robertson and Scott Gorham.

Employing his bass as a third lead instrument, Jack Bruce style, Lynott beefed up the bottom end to make Lizzy metal where contemporaries like Wishbone Ash remained merely rock. They also played host on two occasions to Gary Moore, a fine Irish guitarist who had earlier made his name in Skid Row (not the US band of the same name) and forged an increasingly successful solo career through the 1980s. Lizzy's *Dedication* compilation went gold in 1991 as confirmation of their standing in metal circles.

After Whitesnake, Rainbow was the most successful of the Deep Purple spinoff groups. When saturnine, non-singing axeman Ritchie Blackmore left in 1975, disillusioned with the Purps' new funk-rock direction, he picked up an instant band in the shape of Elf, a US unit led by diminutive singer Ronnie James Dio.

The American's vocals and Blackmore's sweetly stinging guitar were the only constants as the personnel changed bewilderingly, yet their albums were regular British Top Ten entrants. On Dio's departure for Black Sabbath in 1979, Blackmore recruited first Graham Bonnet, then another American, Joe Lynn Turner, to assume the vocalist mantle, and Turner was to rejoin his old boss in the re-formed Deep Purple in 1989 when Ian Gillan was sacked.

Like much in heavy metal, the success of Rainbow suggested that, far from seeking new thrills, the fans were happy to rely on variations on tried and trusted themes. The fact that Deep Purple spun off three successful groups in Gillan, Whitesnake and Rainbow proved that tribal loyalties meant long careers and record sales – a fact the parent group's comeback to Top Ten status in the 1980s only reinforced. Judas Priest's Rob Halford summed it up: 'Heavy metal is not just a passing phase, it's part of your life forever.'

TOP **Rush, Canada's heaviest rock trio, give it all they've got in the persons of guitarist Alex Lifeson (left) and bassist Geddy Lee.**

ABOVE **Lee, Lifeson and (right) drummer Neil Peart, who writes the lyrics for Rush's extravagant creations.**

TOP RIGHT **Ritchie Blackmore's Rainbow display their gold disks. Blackmore stands center, to his left is vocalist Ronnie James Dio, who went on to Black Sabbath and later fronted his own band.**

RIGHT **Ireland's finest, Thin Lizzy (from left) Scott Gorham, Brian Robertson (guitars), Phil Lynott (bass) and Brian Downey (drums).**

THE SEVENTIES SUPERGROUPS

29

THE EIGHTIES NEW WAVE

THE EIGHTIES NEW WAVE

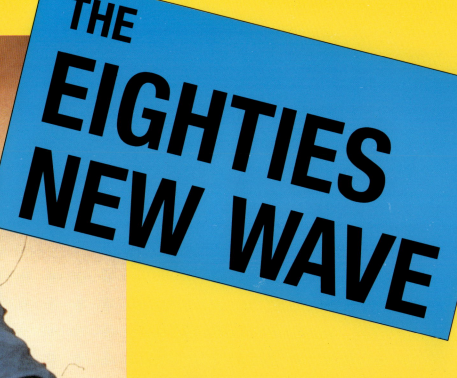

Heavy metal had been a movement which kept its feet firmly on the street. Yet as the 1970s ended and punk rebelled against the prevailing pomp-rock of Yes, Emerson, Lake and Palmer and their ilk, a similar dissatisfaction spread through the HM fraternity. Deep Purple had come and gone, leaving a constellation of mini supergroups in its wake which toured only to push a record release. The next wave of bands like Judas Priest were successful enough to become tax exiles, leaving little or no live music at local level.

The time was ripe for revolution – and up in Sheffield, something mighty was stirring. Def Leppard combined the directness of punk with the musical might of metal . . . and just as the early punk groups had put out their own records, so Leppard combated record companies' lack of interest by releasing an EP, *Getcha Rocks Off*, on their own Bludgeon Riffola label.

On Through The Night was their UK album chart debut in 1980, but it soon became obvious they were going down better in the States. They concentrated on that market and reaped the reward with a string of Top Three singles in the late 1980s from the US-chart-topping album *Hysteria*, including the 1988 Number 1 *Love Bites*.

LEFT Mötley Crüe vocalist Vince Neil socks it to bassist Nikki Sixx as guitarist Mick Mars looks on. Formed in 1981, their 1985 US hit *Smokin' In The Boys' Room* shot them to overnight fame and fortune, though their off-stage dramas with drugs and auto accidents also made headlines.

THE EIGHTIES NEW WAVE

THE EIGHTIES NEW WAVE

The metal magazine *Kerrang!* had earlier hailed 1983's *Pyromania* as 'a milestone . . . the record that helped mold metal in the 1980s, pushing the barriers of songwriting, performance and production to the very limits.' Central to this was Robert 'Mutt' Lange, a producer who first worked with them on 1981's *High and Dry* album and co-wrote all ten *Pyro* tracks. Lange later co-wrote Bryan Adams' 1991 record-breaking single *(Everything I Do) I Do It For You*.

Thanks largely to blond bombshell lead singer Joe Elliott, Leppard's video-friendliness (unlike many HM bands) caused MTV to keep them on heavy rotation to win the hearts and minds of America's youth. Yet they had to survive two tragedies: the first when drummer Rick Allen (a 15-year-old schoolboy on the group's formation) lost his left arm in an auto accident on New Year's Eve 1984 and again when guitarist Steve Clark died after a 1991 drinking spree.

Back in 1977 Leppard weren't the only band with plans for a heavy-metal renaissance. Iron Maiden, Angel Witch, Saxon and others were all plotting and planning their part in what was later to become known as the New Wave of British Heavy Metal. Championed by *Sounds* music paper, they drove a wedge between new wave and the long-established bands and forced themselves into it, ensuring that heavy metal would continue to flourish in the 1980s.

And the most successful of these newcomers was undoubtedly Iron Maiden. Named after a medieval instrument of torture, they were nurtured in the London pub circuit by bass

ABOVE **Iron Maiden's Bruce Dickinson in archetypal heavy-metal pose. His replacement of former singer Paul Di'Anno in 1982 took the London band into metal's major league and lit the fuse for a decade of worldwide success.**

LEFT **Def Leppard (from left) Rick Allen (drums), Joe Elliott (vocals), Steve Clarke (guitar), Rick Savage (bass) and Phil Collen (guitar).**

OPPOSITE **Elliott and Clarke share a tender on-stage moment. The combination of video-friendly looks and hard-rock riffs brought Leppard huge Stateside success. Sadly, Clarke died in 1991.**

THE EIGHTIES NEW WAVE

player/songwriter Steve Harris. Band members came and went, but it wasn't until 1982's chart-topping *Number of The Beast* album, when ex-Samson singer Bruce Dickinson took the vocal reins, that Harris had the line-up to take on the world. The Satanic overtones of the title were tenuous, and Maiden were keen not to stay in a rut: Egyptian imagery took over for 1984's *Powerslave*, bringing in exoticism previously the preserve of the likes of progressive champions Yes. Yet while bands like Def Leppard were bringing romance to metal for the first time, Maiden were of the old school in remaining very much 'men's men.'

The success of *Bring Your Daughter to the Slaughter*, the first UK chart-topping single of 1991, was significant. It was originally written by Dickinson for a *Nightmare On Elm Street* film, underlining the link between metal and the horror-movie genre. And like all Maiden's singles it benefited from the metal fan's obsession with collectable products. Available in picture disk and other limited-edition forms, it invited the 'true fan' to buy it in more than one format, boosting the chances of a Number 1. Maiden's singles inevitably entered high, then sunk inexorably, proving that fans were keen enough to buy in the week of release – and to give the band their due they supplied non-LP bonus tracks to make it worthwhile (the fan would, inevitably, re-purchase the single yet again as a track on the forthcoming album).

Sounds, the music paper behind metal's new wave, spun off the even more influential *Kerrang!* Named after the sound of a guitar power chord, it was, and still is, the metal fan's bible. Yet there were forces ranged against the music – notably the US Parents Music Resource Center, a pressure group keen to censor music they considered harmful to youth. Frank Zappa was among those opposed to these moves and said so in a Senate subcommittee in Washington in the late 1980s. Most of the censors' proposals were defeated, though stickering of albums containing 'offensive language' was a watered-down end result. Yet even this had a positive effect in stressing the appeal of the forbidden. Christian rock was a less conventional attempt to save the youth of the world, with Stryper coming nearest to proving the Devil didn't have all the best tunes.

Apart from Golden Earring, the Netherlands had contributed little to rock history. Yet Dutch-born Eddie Van Halen and drumming brother Alex were to change all that – albeit many thousands of miles from their Nijmegen birthplace. The duo were brought up on the Californian coast, and met drama student-turned-singer Dave Lee Roth at high school. Within weeks they were playing the club scene: not long after guitarist Eddie's 21st birthday, they'd hit the stadium circuit with a vengeance after being discovered by Kiss's Gene Simmons.

The combination of extrovert showman Dave Lee Roth and Eddie's inventive axework reached rather further than the front row of the stalls: his technique on Van Halen's first self-named long player inspired Roth to comment: 'Eddie Van Halen is the first guitar hero of the Eighties: all the other guitar heroes are dead.' That was in 1978. Five years later, he swept the board when prestigious *Guitar Player* magazine polled the world's major rock guitarists to nominate their favorite player. Then in 1983 they made the record books with a $1.5 million payday for appearing at the US Festival – a cool $16,000 a minute!

ABOVE Eddie Van Halen and his distinctive guitar have been a dominant sight and sound in metal for well over a decade, his style winning him the admiration of fans and respect of his fellow musicians.

RIGHT David Lee Roth, former frontman for the group Van Halen who quit in 1985 for a successful solo career. One of his early line-ups featured another stunning axeman in Steve Vai.

THE EIGHTIES NEW WAVE

35

THE EIGHTIES NEW WAVE

LEFT Saxon vocalist Biff Byford takes the acclaim of another satisfied crowd. The Yorkshiremen have proved a big live attraction on the UK metal circuit for the past decade and a half.

RIGHT The inimitable Motorhead bassist/vocalist Ian 'Lemmy' Kilminster, who swapped Hawkwind's space rock for his own brand of speed metal in the mid-1970s . . . and hasn't slowed down yet!

BELOW RIGHT Birmingham metal veterans Magnum (from left) Wally Lowe (bass), Mark Stanway (keyboards), Bob Catley (vocals), Mickey Barker (drums) and Tony 'The Hat' Clarkin (guitar).

Their initial weakness was in the songwriting department, their fourth LP, 1982's *Diver Down* (the third to go Top Ten) comprising one third covers. But the chart-topping success of *Jump* a single from 1984's *MCMLXXXIV* was not only a VH original but their first major track to feature not guitar but . . . gasp! . . . synthesizer! The same year Eddie iced Michael Jackson's soul-rock crossover *Beat It* with the perfect guitar solo, proving he hadn't lost the knack.

Roth's departure the following year for a solo career never threatened Van Halen's equilibrium: indeed Eddie showed consummate confidence in recruiting ex-Montrose frontman Sammy Hagar, himself no mean player, to add even more bite to the front line. More big American hits followed with *Why Can't This Be Love* and *When It's Love*.

Never afraid to court controversy – witness *MCMLXXXIV*'s cigarette-smoking cherub and 1991's acronymically-titled *For Unlawful Carnal Knowledge* – Van Halen gave the lie to the oft-repeated cliché that heavy metal had no sense of humor. Bassist Michael Anthony summed up their appeal: 'It's about what everybody feels on a Friday or Saturday night. You come home from work or school, you have your bath, you shave, you jump in your car, you pick up your girlfriend and you're gonna have a good time. Well, with Van Halen *every* night's a Saturday night.'

Sweden put in its own bid for heavy-metal world domination when Europe raced to Number 1 in 14 countries with the symphonic, keyboard-led splendor of *The Final Countdown*. They were never able to equal their 1986 impact despite a number of impressive (and much heavier, guitar-based) follow-up tracks. Lead singer Joey Tempest's Scandinavian good looks brought acclaim from teenage girls and led to acceptance problems with some of the fan fraternity, though a US tour with Def Leppard ensured no confusion in the States.

British band Saxon were the 1980s' equivalent of Uriah Heep and Budgie – hard working and little recognized outside their own fan following. Formed in Yorkshire in 1977, the band fronted by Biff Byford and featuring the twin-guitar attack of Graham Oliver and Paul Quinn established themselves as working-class heroes through solid touring. A 1979 support stint for Motorhead saw the headliners' career take off and Saxon's *Wheels Of Steel* follow them into the Top Five. Their forte, too, was the hit single, clocking up 15 *Guinness Book of Hit Singles*' entries in the 1980s including a metallic cover of Christopher Cross's *Ride Like The Wind*. Though Saxon's efforts were melodic enough for mainstream radio infiltration, the airwaves were now alive with specialist rock shows, British DJs like Tommy Vance and Alan Freeman among the mainstays.

Birmingham five-piece Magnum were beneficiaries of this upswing, having toured every venue known to man since their 1976 formation by ever-present vocalist Bob Catley and guitarist/songwriter Tony Clarkin. Specializing in the metal tradition of sword and sorcery themes (their cover artist Rodney Matthews ranked close to Roger Dean in devising prime-metal packaging)

THE EIGHTIES NEW WAVE

they remained a hard-working cult until the self-funded *On A Storyteller's Night* proved a surprise hit on the FM label in 1985. Signed to Polydor, a Donington appearance and the patronage of Queen's Roger Taylor who initially produced them, they came good with the 1988 Top Five album *Wings of Heaven*.

'If we moved in next door, your lawn would shrivel up!' threatened Motorhead leader Ian 'Lemmy' Kilminster when he founded the ultimate power trio. The definitive three-piece line-up of Lemmy (bass, vocals), 'Fast' Eddie Clarke (guitar) and Phil 'Philthy Animal' Taylor (drums), produced a pioneering brand of music that laid the foundations for speed-metal merchants like Anthrax and Metallica to build on later. Lemmy, formerly of space-rockers Hawkwind, named his band after the American slang for 'speed-freak,' and their brand of music often led in the early days to appearances on punk-rock bills, promoters mistaking them for a new wave band.

The 1979 albums *Overkill* and *Bomber* made the breakthrough after a false start, while 1981's definitive live statement *No Sleep Till Hammersmith* topped the UK chart.

THE EIGHTIES NEW WAVE

Mention of Motorhead brings in labelmates Girlschool, who shared a Top Five EP with them in 1981 though never established themselves in as big a way.

David Coverdale's contribution to the Deep Purple story must rate second to that of Ian Gillan, the man he replaced – but Whitesnake, his post-Purple effort, must rank as the most successful spinoff. Like Ritchie Blackmore, he rang the changes personnel-wise, racking up six albums by 1982 (the first two of which were officially solo efforts). Critics made much of the presence of Jon Lord and Ian Paice, calling 'Whitesnake 'Purple in disguise,' while the anti-sexist lobby derided the 'nude girl astride a giant python' logo.

An unrepentant Coverdale continued pushing his self-professed 'cock rock,' commencing a swift rise to supergroup status with a 1983 headliner at Donington and the following year's *Slide It In*. It was a measure of his success that when Lord quit to re-form Purple, Coverdale had nothing to fear from comparisons. 1989's *Slip Of The Tongue* was his seventh successive UK Top Ten album, and reflected a fruitful writing partnership with guitarist Adrian Vandenberg, though 1991 saw him link with ex-Zeppelin *axemeister* Jimmy Page.

ABOVE **London's Girlschool, whose energetic blend of new-wave energy and metal brought them a keen live following but failed to sustain success on record.**

ABOVE RIGHT **The irrepressible David Coverdale (center), who remains unapologetic for his group Whitesnake's somewhat unliberated approach to sexual politics.**

RIGHT **Ozzy Osbourne, who proved there was life after Black Sabbath by producing a string of successful solo albums in the 1980s despite battling with alcohol and drug problems.**

THE EIGHTIES NEW WAVE

Ozzy Osbourne was another ex-lead singer to break big in the 1980s in his own right. He'd released two albums (*Blizzard Of Ozz* in 1980, and *Diary Of A Madman* in 1981) after leaving Black Sabbath, but it was his third solo effort, *Talk Of The Devil*, that showed he had a future – ironically with an album that contained nothing but Black Sabbath songs. He'd been making headlines for all the wrong reasons, like problems with drink/drugs and the death of guitarist Randy Rhoads in March 1982 after buzzing the tour bus in a light airplane, but the live album – a contractual obligation to his previous manager – put him back on the map. It reached the US Number 14 position (at that time his best solo showing) and Number 21 in Britain. He continued to sell records and make headlines (urinating on the Alamo, reputedly biting the head off a bat on stage) through the decade.

As Osbourne demonstrated, heavy-metal acts are nothing if not nonconformist, but Texan trio ZZ Top were more original than most. With an image that consisted initially of long beards and 12-bar blues boogie, they created their own niche, returning after a three-year recording break to become one of the 1980s' surprise successes. With a line-up of Billy Gibbons (guitar), Dusty Hill (bass) and Frank Beard (drums, ironically the only beardless

THE EIGHTIES NEW WAVE

LEFT ZZ Top guitarist Billy Gibbons spanks his plank. His band's line-up has remained unchanged over 21 years and numerous hit albums.

ABOVE WASP's provocative stance against the forces of authority – as exemplified by ever-present Blackie Lawless – ensured them a passionate worldwide following.

ABOVE RIGHT Chris Holmes of WASP, the other stalwart in the band's changing line-up.

THE EIGHTIES NEW WAVE

band member!) that had remained stable since their 1970 formation, they were remembered mainly for 1975's much-covered *Tush* – but their 1980s rebirth added a string of glossy hits to their roll of honor, all embellished by promotional videos that simultaneously celebrated and sent up their weird 'n' wacky lifestyle. The catalyst was 1983's *Eliminator*, a stunning amalgamation of synthesizers and drum machines into Top's age-old formula. The result was the hits *Legs, Gimme All Your Lovin', TV Dinners* and *Sharp Dressed Man*.

The new medium of the promotional video was offering 1980s bands unlimited scope for promoting their image. Many chose to stick with live film footage, but WASP were among those who made capital from the video. They burst on to the scene in 1983, their initials representing either White Anglo Saxon Protestants or (more likely) We Are Sexual Perverts, they were picked up by Iron Maiden's management and proceeded to shock the unshockable. The record company Capitol refused to release their debut single *Animal (F*ck Like A Beast)*, which subsequently appeared on the independent Music For Nations label, shifting a healthy 130,000 copies. From then on, WASP buzzed onwards with a hat-trick of million-selling albums. Personnel problems seemed to matter little, with bassist/guitarist Blackie Lawless and guitarist Chris Holmes the constant factors.

They took on the PMRC, suing them for using a WASP single sleeve without permission, and released the theme to the film *Ghoulies II* with an accompanying horror video. Then *The Headless Children*, their fourth studio album, rocketed them to a higher level and took them into the British Top Ten.

THE EIGHTIES NEW WAVE

Los Angeles' Mötley Crüe also took time to make the breakthrough: in their case, it was 1989's *Dr Feelgood* that topped the *Decade of Decadence* they were to celebrate two years later. 'We're like a magnet for trouble,' claimed their bassist Nikki Sixx – and he should know, having lain dead for two minutes after a heroin overdose in 1988. Further complications ensued when one Matthew Trippe sued the band's management, claiming he'd filled in for Sixx when the bassist (real name Frank Farrano) was allegedly in jail. Add drummer Tommy Lee's stormy marriage with *Dynasty* soap star Heather Locklear and a fatal December 1984 auto accident involving vocalist Vince Neil and you had a band which one reviewer dubbed 'Another excuse for Mums to lock up their teenage daughters.' Another tagged their music and image as 'a raucous amalgam of Kiss and the New York Dolls.'

Despite only the occasional hit single (*Smokin' In The Boys' Room, Girls Girls Girls*), the band inspired many US males to take the metal road, Skid Row being just one. 'Journalists can write what they please . . . when they stop writing about us, that's when I'll worry.' Despite their hard-living image, 1989's success coincided with a rejection of their former ways. 'We're experimenting with music as opposed to drugs,' claimed Lee.

Another LA band, Quiet Riot, had enjoyed brief fame in 1983 when their *Metal Health* topped the US chart – a first for a debut metal album and something bands as big as Kiss never once managed. The key was a cover of British band Slade's *Cum On Feel The Noize*, a track most UK metallurgists would have considered pop. Two further hit albums followed before gravel-voiced singer Kevin DuBrow left in 1987.

The 1980s saw the evolution of the festival as an almost exclusively heavy-metal preserve. In the 1960s, Woodstock,

THE EIGHTIES NEW WAVE

ABOVE AND ABOVE LEFT Los Angeles' Mötley Crüe have overcome many problems in their 10-year existence to emerge as one of America's hottest, heaviest bands.

OVERLEAF Quiet Riot invite you to *Feel The Noize* in 1984. The band topped the US chart with their debut LP *Metal Health* but success was to prove brief.

Monterey and their ilk were oases of peace, love and harmony amidst an uncaring world. At Altamont all that changed when a Rolling Stones fan was shot by Hell's Angels as, unaware of the situation, the band played on.

Thankfully, Altamont was the exception rather than the rule. But Status Quo's appearance at Britain's Reading Festival in 1972 proved a forerunner of things to come: by the 1980s, the event was an exclusively heavy-metal occasion. In the States, the huge US Festival played host to Van Halen and their like, while in Britain the Monsters of Rock festival at Castle Donington became *the* event to headline. In 1988 two fans died in a crowd accident as Guns N' Roses played on oblivious, raising long-forgotten memories – but in an age of compact disks and adult-orientated rock, it was arguably only real enthusiasts who would sit in a muddy field for hours on end having their senses assaulted.

THE EIGHTIES NEW WAVE

THE EIGHTIES NEW WAVE

THE FUTURE

46

THE FUTURE

Heavy metal in the 1990s occupied a place as close to the mainstream as it had ever enjoyed. With the advent of the compact disk, classic 1970s material was resurfacing to delight another generation: Led Zeppelin's *Remasters* compilations even made the UK Top Ten albums in 1990!

Metal had finally recognized that women could get into the music, too. Surprisingly, however, few women had broken into the genre in a performing sense. Canadian Lee Aaron, ex-Runaways guitarist Lita Ford and UK singer Lisa Dominique all made valiant attempts but failed to make a lasting impression.

Hailing from New Jersey, Bon Jovi managed to take the crown as the heavy-metal band most fans' sisters would like to date. With photogenic frontmen Jon Bon Jovi (vocals) and Richie Sambora (guitar) they charmed press and public, while even the most hardened rocker had to warm to such anthemic cuts as *You Give Love A Bad Name* and *Livin' On A Prayer* – both 1986 US chart-toppers from the US Number 1 LP *Slippery When Wet*. (The album's eight-week stay at the top beat Led Zeppelin's long-standing heavy-metal record.)

LEFT Bon Jovi's front line (from left) lead guitarist Richie Sambora, vocalist Jon Bon Jovi and bassist Alec Jon Such. A combination of good looks and great music saw the East Coast outfit emerge from the metal scene to conquer the pop charts in the late 1980s with a series of crossover hits and Number 1 albums such as *Slippery When Wet*.

THE FUTURE

The band was dealt a blow when manager Doc McGhee was arrested on drugs charges, but turned even this to their advantage, making headlines worldwide with 1989's anti-drug Make A Difference Festival, staged in pre-*perestroika* Moscow. On the recording front, they attempted to put one foot into the adult rock circles inhabited by neighbor Bruce Springsteen with their fourth LP, 1988's *New Jersey*, but sacrificed a degree of commercial success in the process (it topped the UK and US album chart nevertheless). With press attention centering on Jon Bon Jovi's business activities with management/production company The Underground, they took a break: guitarist Sambora distanced himself by recording a solo album, while Jon himself cut a hit film theme *Blaze of Glory*, insisting the band would re-form in the near future.

If Bon Jovi represented the acceptable face of metal, Los Angeles' Guns N' Roses most certainly did not. The self-styled 'Most Dangerous Band in the World' burst on to the world stage in 1988, mixing their brand of glam-metal with a decidedly punk-like attitude. They challenged public morals with their blatant album covers, aggressive titles and angry lyrics. Well-publicized drugs problems dogged them, their drummer being sacked for indulging – then threatening to sue them for encouraging his habit. Concerts ended in riots, once with a knife-wielding fan on stage. Yet the aura of excess that surrounded the band made them worldwide front-page news.

ABOVE Jon Bon Jovi flies the flag. Of Italian immigrant parents, he helped Bruce Springsteen put New Jersey on the music map.

RIGHT 1990s' nightmares Guns N' Roses (from left) Axl Rose, Duff McKagan, Slash, Izzy Stradlin and Steven Adler.

LEFT Lita Ford, previously lead guitarist with new wave group the Runaways (who also featured Joan Jett), made her first solo mark in metal with the US hit single *Kiss Me Deadly* in 1988.

THE FUTURE

THE FUTURE

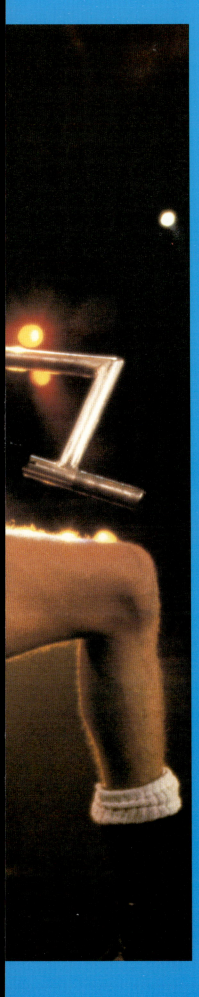

LEFT AND ABOVE Axl Rose's wild and crazy on-stage antics – he was once arrested in mid set – have drawn more attention than anyone in rock since the Doors' Jim Morrison. Nevertheless, he typifies the band's 'on the edge' image which has made them metal's megaband of the 1990s.

THE FUTURE

LEFT Anthrax singer Joey Belladonna (who replaced original vocalist Neil Turbin) hits the high notes with guitarist Dan Spitz.

RIGHT The other Anthrax axeman, Scott Ian, models a neat line in beachwear. Original and uncompromising, the band are deservedly leaders of their chosen thrash-metal genre.

Lead singer Axl Rose followed guitar-playing schoolmate Jeff Isabelle (aka Izzy Stradlin) to Los Angeles in 1980, where the duo wrote songs together as the nucleus of Hollywood Rose. A merger with fellow bar-band LA Guns and bass player Duff (Michael) McKagan produced Guns N' Roses, and the definitive line-up resulted with the addition of Slash (real name Saul Hudson, guitar) and Steven Adler (drums). Signing to Geffen in early 1986, the following year's *Appetite For Destruction* combined the power of metal with the rebellion of punk. A succession of support tours propelled it to the top of the US charts in the summer of 1988 – only the second heavy-metal debut album ever to achieve the feat, and that 50 weeks after release. *Sweet Child O' Mine* also made Guns N' Roses only the fifth hard-rock band in history to score a US Number 1 single.

The follow-up album, 1988's *G N' R Lies*, was an earlier home-made EP, augmented and repackaged. On release *Lies* made Guns N' Roses the first band in the 1980s to have two simultaneous albums in the US Top Five.

Drummer Steven Adler left in July 1990, allegedly with a drug problem that was affecting his playing. Replacement Matt Sorum from the Cult joined, along with unknown keyboardist Dizzy Read, to appear on *Use Your Illusion*, finally released in September 1991 as two double albums.

The lyrical content was as direct as ever, and even the cautionary sticker on the front of the sleeve contained offensive language, and resulted in certain chain stores refusing to stock the album. Nevertheless *Illusion*'s two volumes entered the UK and US album charts in reverse order at Number 1 and 2 – just as founder member Izzy put in his notice to quit.

If bands like Bon Jovi recognized a woman's right to rock, so speed and thrash metal redressed the balance with rituals almost akin to hooliganism. Slamdancing and moshing, two terms for what in the 1970s would have been termed 'idiot dancing,' were integral to its enjoyment. Anthrax and Metallica were two of the leading lights of the genre, ahead of Megadeth and Slayer.

Anthrax, whose *Caught In A Mosh* is one of the definitive thrash tracks, later attempted to forge an unlikely alliance with rap music, a collaboration with Chuck D on Public Enemy's *Bring The Noise*, reminiscent of the Run DMC/Aerosmith teaming on *Walk This Way*. This funk/metal path was also being followed by the Red Hot Chili Peppers, Faith No More and the Dan Reed Network, suggesting a new direction for metal in the 1990s.

THE FUTURE

THE FUTURE

Not that Anthrax needed to jump on any bandwagons. Their first recording was in 1983, but not until the original vocalist was replaced by Joey Belladonna for 1985's *Armed And Dangerous* EP did the upward climb begin in earnest – and as Anthrax climbed, so did thrash metal.

Drummer Charlie Benante revealed the band's source of inspiration. 'When I was younger and everyone else was into Van Halen, I was always into other stuff like Motorhead.' They resented being pigeonholed to such an extent that they covered a Joe Jackson track *Got The Time* for a 1990 hit. But, as guitarist Scott Ian emphasized, 'it's not good unless the stuff is coming out of the speakers so loud it's blowin' your hair back.' As ever, the sound and fury, not the lyrics, were paramount.

BELOW **Metallica lead singer James Hetfield thunders out another show-stopping song.**

RIGHT **Drummer Lars Ulrich, who founded Metallica in 1981 as an American counterpart to the British new wave of bands. In 1991, his outfit's fifth album entered the UK charts at the very top, emphasizing the band's impact and influence in the intervening decade.**

THE FUTURE

55

THE FUTURE

LEFT **Extreme (from left) Gary Cherone, Paul Geary, Nuno Bettencourt and Pat Badger.**

RIGHT **Living Colour (from left) Vernon Reid, William Calhoun, Corey Glover, and Muzz Skillings, have proved by their success that there's no color bar to making classic metal.**

BELOW RIGHT **Black Crowe frontman Chris Robinson in Rod Stewart-lookalike mode. Though hailing from Georgia, the Crowes were heavily influenced by British acts of the 1970s like Free and the Faces.**

Inspired by the British New Wave of Heavy Metal, Metallica's uncompromising drummer Lars Ulrich (one of the few sticksmen to lead HM bands) formed his outfit with guitarist James Hetfield in San Francisco in 1981. For the longest time they were renowned in the music business as the band that refused *point blank* to shoot a video. They fed the legend by releasing a budget EP of cover versions and titling it *$5.98* so greedy shop owners couldn't rip off their fans for more, touring every US state (including Alaska!) and carrying on after the tragic tour death of original bassist Cliff Burton because 'we know it's what he would've wanted,' He was replaced by bassist Jason Newsted, while lead guitarist Kirk Hammett made up the team.

With its totally black cover and anonymous title, 1991's fifth album *Metallica* took them higher than ever, entering the UK chart at Number 1. And the free album premieres at British venues with video footage thrown in contrasted strongly with heavy-metal merchandizing which, by the 1990s, had gone off the deep end with everything from patches and scarves to condoms available with your favorite band's logo affixed. The all-black packaging too, was a reaction to over-elaborate album covers: a statement that the music still came first and foremost. Metallica had, however, broken an eight-year vow not to do videos – and by collaborating with Bon Jovi producer Bob Rock they had brought their sound up to date and outgrown the 'thrash metal' label without compromising their own ideals.

The 1990s scene saw many revivals: Bon Jovi played Thin Lizzy's *The Boys Are Back In Town* as an encore number, sparking interest in the 1970s giants, while veterans like American axeman Joe Walsh (who traded in his promising metal beginnings to join the Eagles in the 1970s) were still treading the boards and recording.

Yet if heavy metal originated in Britain, it was refreshing to see Thunder, a new British band, go gold with their first album, 1990's *Back Street Symphony* and score four Top Forty singles in the process. They went down well in the States too, suggesting them as brightest British hopes for the 1990s.

The US chart-topping ballad *More Than Words* brought Boston's Extreme to public attention for the first time. Yet the band had been paying their dues for six years previously and amounted to rather more than an overnight success.

THE FUTURE

Singer Gary Cherone and Portuguese-born guitarist extraordinaire Nuno Bettencourt were the obvious focal points – something the band acknowledged tongue in cheek with the rhythm section of bassist Pat Badger and drummer Paul Geary 'lighter-waving' on the video in which only Cherone and Bettencourt actually perform. The band was formed in 1985 from two separate Boston outfits. Their first, self-named album was dogged by bad luck, but the double platinum *Pornograffiti*, released in 1990, became one of rock's great 'sleeper' successes. Since then, Nuno Bettencourt has realized every axeman's dream – to have an instrument named after him – and the sky seems the limit for a band which, like Bon Jovi, is easy on the eye but uncompromising in its musical outlook.

If Jimi Hendrix proved that there was no color bar in metal, few were taking up the challenge until Living Colour broke through in 1990 with their second album *Time's Up*. Mick Jagger had been one of their most fervent supporters, and it was on a bill with the Stones and Guns N' Roses that trouble flared when the New York quartet publicly registered their objection to Axl Rose's racist lyric to *One In A Million*. Their hard-edged rock with a touch of

THE FUTURE

humor made them a band to watch irrespective of skin color, with actor-turned-singer Corey Glover and virtuoso jazz-trained guitarist Vernon Reid their main men. With two platinum albums to their credit, they could shape the future of heavy metal by making it something for black America (and Britain) to aspire to.

Atlanta's Black Crowes hit the headlines when they were removed from their 'special guest' slot on ZZ Top's 1991 US tour for derogatory comments about tour sponsors Miller beer. Singer Chris Robinson had no regrets. 'I'm guilty of just one thing,' he complains, 'having different priorities. We're still angry and we're still sexy and we're still dangerous and we're still trying to prove something.'

Pulling their inspiration from the golden age of 1970s rock, Robinson and guitarist brother Rich injected a 1990s energy. The band got through three drummers and six bassists before settling on a rhythm section – the others just didn't have the commitment the Robinson brothers demanded.

The Crowes had cut the mega-selling 1990 debut *Shake Your Money Maker* on a low budget, using the proceeds of their advance from record label Def American. Over a year later, it was still selling in chart-worthy quantities of three million and rising. And it was all achieved with a notable lack of image.

By contrast, Poison represented the possibility that style could triumph over substance. Hailing from Harrisburg, Pennsylvania, they pooled their possessions and sold them to gamble on their future, changing their name from Paris en route and arriving in LA with a fabled $42 between them! Their debut album *Look What The Cat Dragged In* represented Harrisburg's attitude to their Spandex 'n' hairspray appearance, but the laugh was on them when *Every Rose Has Its Thorn* topped the US charts in late 1988 and stayed there for five weeks. Singer Bret Michaels, who overcame diabetes to get to the top, had the last laugh. 'The first impression of us was that we were a pansy band,' he admitted, 'It turns out to be the opposite.'

THE FUTURE

ABOVE Poison guitarist CC Deville (real name Bruce Johannsson) was a film director before devoting his life to the metal cause.

LEFT The Black Crowes in an off-duty moment. Their 1991 worldwide success was achieved with a deliberate lack of image, as can readily be believed!

RIGHT Despite appearances, Poison vocalist Bret Michaels overcame the handicap of being diagnosed a diabetic to reach the top of the rock tree.

OVERLEAF Poison camp it up. 'You can call us Glam, Metal, Rock, anything you want,' says singer Bret Michaels (third from left), 'as long as people come out and take a listen.'

THE FUTURE

ABOVE AND RIGHT Sebastian Bach, frontman and face of 1991 US chart-toppers Skid Row. Coming to prominence under the patronage of Bon Jovi, the band went on to establish themselves as chart-toppers in their own right with their 1991 album *Slave To The Grind*.

Another band with plenty of image was Skid Row. Fronted by pretty boy Sebastian Bach, they enjoyed a rocket ride to fame and fortune courtesy of a five-million-selling first album (1988's *Skid Row*), an appearance at the historic Makes A Difference Festival in Moscow and a much-publicized signing to Bon Jovi's management/production company The Underground (they've since left).

But with 17 months on the road, Skid Row took their time producing 1991's *Slave To The Grind* – and all doubts were allayed when the album debuted at Number 1 in the States, the first album to do so since Michael Jackson's *Bad* in 1987.

The dark, brooding record contrasted strongly with the upbeat optimism of the first platter. Touring had brought mixed fortunes: a bottle-throwing incident during which a fan sustained an injury requiring six stitches saw Bach in the dock. Skid Row returned to the road in 1991 as support act to Guns N' Roses, still looking to prove their right to be regarded as 1990s' greats.

And if the early 1990s were anything to go by, it would be a decade which would find heavy metal not only alive but thriving. The media was quick to keep pace: once the undisputed flagship of heavy rock magazines, *Kerrang!* was challenged by the likes of *RAW*, *Metal Forces*, *Metal Hammer* and *Rock Power*. The last two were both pan-European ventures, and *Rock Power* was even circulating in Russia, proving metal's appeal to be as universal as ever.

'Heavy metal is the basic rock'n'roll message,' says *Rock World* editor John Swenson. 'It accepts everybody. The least sophisticated kid can get as much out of it as dedicated followers.' The number of those followers seems greater and more widespread than ever.

But where could the music go from here? Could it get louder, prouder, lyrics more explicit, stage acts more shocking? The answer was no . . . and yes. As genres like thrash metal, once radical, became part of the mainstream, so kids at street level investigated more 'way-out' trends as hardcore (a tuneless throwback to punk from US groups like Agnostic Front) and death metal (which could perhaps be described as Black Sabbath for a new generation from Napalm Death and Obituary). Fans of these groups would doubtless regard even Guns N' Roses as 'middle of the road.'

Yet what appears at first glance to be fragmentation is all part of heavy metal evolving and growing, girding its loins for a new century of challenge. If the genre had been accepted by the rock establishment, it had done its bit in changing the face of rock music after shoving its foot in a fast-closing door. Heavy metal is here to stay – no matter what!

INDEX AND ACKNOWLEDGMENTS

Index

Page numbers in *italics* refer to illustrations

Aaron, Lee 47
AC/DC 21, *21*
Adams, Bryan 33
Adler, Steven *49*, 52
Aerosmith 27, *27*, 52
Agnostic Front 62
Allen, Rick 33, *33*
Altamont festival 43
Amboy Dukes 24
Angel Witch 33
Anthony, Michael 36
Anthrax 37, 52, *52-3*, 54
Atomic Rooster trio 10

Bach, Sebastian 62, *62-3*
Bachman, Randy 27, 28
Bachman Turner Overdrive 27, 28
Badger, Pat *56*, 57
Baker, Ginger 7, *8*
Baldwin, John *see* Jones, John Paul
Beard, Frank 39
Beck, Jeff 7, 8, 10, 18, *18*
Beck, Bogert and Appice group 8
Belladonna, Joey *52*, 54
Benante, Charlie 54
Bettencourt, Nuno *56*, 57
Billion Dollar Babies 18
Black Crowes 18, *57*, 58, *58*
Black Sabbath 5, 12, *12*, 17, 28, 39, 62
Blackmore, Ritchie 20, *20*, 28, *29*, 38
Blades, Jack 24
Bogert, Tim 8, *8*
Bon Jovi 27, *46*, 47, 49, 52, 56, 57
Bonham, Jason *14*
Bonham, John 15, 17
Bonnet, Graham 28
Box, Mick 22
Brown, Arthur 10, *10*
Bruce, Jack 7, *8*, 28
Budgie band 23, 36
Burton, Cliff 56
Butler, Terry 'Geezer' 12, *12*
Byford, Bill 36, *36*
Byron, David 22, *22*

Carr, Eric 27
Catley, Bob 36, *37*
Cherone, Gary *56*, 57
Clapton, Eric 7, *7-8*, 10
Clark, Steve *32-3*, 33
Clarke, 'Fast' Eddie 37
Clarkin, Tony 'The Hat' 36, *37*
Cooper, Alice (Vincent Furnier) 18, *18*, 24
Coverdale, David 5, 38, *39*
Crane, Vincent 10, *10-11*
Cream 7, *8*, 12
Criss, Peter 27
Cross, Christopher 36

Dall, Bobby *1*
Damn Yankees group 24
Dan Reed Network 52
Dean, Roger 36
Deep Purple 8, 17, 20, 28, 31, 38
Def Leppard 31, *32-3*, 33, 34, 36
Deville, CC *1*, *59*
Dickinson, Bruce *33*, 34
Dio, Ronnie James 28, *29*
Dominique, Lisa 47
Donington festival 27, 43
DuBrow, Kevin 42, *44*

Earth (Black Sabbath) 12

Elliott, Joe *32-3*, 33
Extreme 18, *56*, 56-7

Farrano, Frank *see* Sixx, Nicki
Ford, Lita 47, *48*
Frampton, Peter 27
Freeman, Alan 36
Freshley, Ace 27
Furnier, Vincent *see* Cooper, Alice

Geary, Paul *56*, 57
Gibbons, Billy 39, *40*
Gillan, Ian 20, *20*, 28, 38
Girlschool 38, *38*
Glover, Corey *57*, 58
Glover, Roger 20, *20*
Gorham, Scott 28, *29*
Guns N' Roses 5, 18, 27, 43, 49, *49*, 52, 57, 62
GWAR 18

Hagar, Sammy 36
Halford, Rob 21, 22, 28
Hammett, Kirk 56
Harris, Steve 34
Hendrix, Jimi 7, 8, *9*, 10, 28, 57
Hensley, Ken 22
Hetfield, James *54*, 56
Hill, Dusty 39
Holmes, Chris 41, *41*
Howe, Steve 8
Hudson, Saul *see* Slash
Hughes, Glenn 20

Ian, Scott *53*, 54
Iommi, Tony 12, *12*
Iron Maiden 33-4, 41
Isabelle, Jeff *see* Stradlin, Izzy

Jackson, Joe 54
Jackson, Michael 36, 62
Jagger, Mick 27, 57
Jeff Beck 10, *18*
Johnson, Brian 21
Jones, John Paul *14*, 15, *16*
Jovi, Jon Bon *46*, 47, 49, *49*, 62
Judas Priest *21*, 22, 28, 31

Kay, John *9*
Kerslake, Lee 22
Kilminster, Ian 'lemmy' 37, *37*
Kiss 18, 24, 25, *25*, 27, 34, 42

LA Guns 52
Lange, Robert 'Mutt' 33
Lawless, Blackie *40*, 41
Led Zeppelin 10, *14*, 15, *16-17*, 17, 47
Lee, Alvin 18, *18*
Lee, Geddy 28, *28*
Lee, Tommy 42
Lennon, John 18
Lifeson, Alex *28*
Living Colour *57*, 57-8
Locklear, Heather 42
Lord, Jon 20, *20*, 38
Lowe, Wally 37
Lynott, Phil 28, *29*

Magnum band 36-7, *37*
Make A Difference Festival, Moscow 49, 62
Mars, Mick 30
Martinez, Paul 17
Matthews, Rodney 36
McGhee, Doc 49
McKagan, Duff (Michael) *49*, 52
Meat Loaf 23, *23*, 24
Megadeth 52
Meine, Klaus 22
Metallica 37, 52, *54*, 56
Michael Schenke 22
Michaels, Bret *1*, 58, *59-60*
Mogg, Phil 22, 23

Monterey festival 43
Moon, Keith 15
Moore, Gary 28
Mötley Crüe 18, *30*, 42, *42-3*
Motorhead 36, 37, *37*, 38, 54
Mountain 12, *13*

Neil, Vince *30*, 42
New Yardbirds (Led Zeppelin, *qv*) 15
Newstead, Jason 56
Nugent, Ted 24, *24*

Oliver, Graham 36
Osbourne, John 'Ozzy' *2-3*, 12, *12*, 18, 39, *39*

Page, Jimmy 7, 10, *14*, 15, *16*, 18, 38
Paice, Ian *20*, 38
Pappalardi, Felix 12
Parfitt, Rick *13*
Parker, Andy 22
Peart, Neil 28
Perry, Joe 27, *27*
Pink Floyd band 10
Plant, Robert 'Percy' *14*, 15, 17, *17*
Poison *1*, 58, *59-61*

Queen 22, 37
Quiet Riot 42, *44*
Quinn, Paul 36

Rainbow 28, *29*
Read, Dizzy 52
Reid, Vernon *57*, 58
Rhoads, Randy 39
Robertson, Brian 28, *29*
Robinson, Chris *57*, 58
Robinson, Rich 58
Rock, Bob 56
Rockett, Rikki *1*
Rolling Stones 18, 27, 43, 57
Rose, Axl *5*, *49-51*, 52, 57
Roth, David Lee 34, *35*, 36
Roth, Uli John 22
Rush 28, *28*

Sambora, Richie *46*, 47, 49
Satriani, Joe 18
Savage, Rick 33
Saxon 33, 36, *36*
Schenker, Michael 22-3
Schenker, Rudolf 22
Scorpions 20, 22, 23
Scott, Bon 21
Shaw, Tommy 24
Simmons, Gene 24, *25-6*, 27, 34
Sixx, Nikki *30*, 42
Skid Row 62, *62-3*
Skillings, Muzz 57
Slade 9, 42
Slash (Saul Hudson) *49*, 52
Slayer 18
Sorum, Matt 52
Spitz, Dan 52
Springsteen, Bruce 49
Stanley, Paul 25, 27
Stanway, Mark 37
Status Quo 12, *13*, 43
Stein, Mark 8
Steinman, Jim 23
Steppenwolf 8, *9*
Stewart, Rod 18, *18*
Stradlin, Izzy *49*, 52
Such, Alec Jon *46*
Swenson, John 62

Taylor, Phil 'Philthy Animal' 37
Taylor, Roger 37
Tempest, Joey 36
Ten Years After 18, *18*
Thain, Gary 22
Thin Lizzy 28, *29*, 56
Thompson, Tony 17

Thornton, Blair 27
Thunder 56
Trippe, Matthew 42
Turner, Joe Lynn 28
Twisted Sister 18
Tyler, Steve 27, *27*

UFO 22-3, *23*
Uriah Heep 22, *22*, 36
Urich, Lars *54*, 56

Va, Steve 18, 34
Van Halen, Alex 34
Van Halen, Eddie 34, *34*, 36
Van Halen 20, 22, 34, 36, 43, 54
Vance, Tommy 36
Vanda, Harry 21
Vandenberg, Adrian *4*, 38
Vanilla Fudge 8, *8*, 20
Vincent, Vinnie 27

Waller, Micky *18*
Walsh, Joe 56
Ward, Bill 12, *12*
WASP *40-41*, 41
Way, Pete 22, 23, *23*
West, Leslie 12, *13*
Wheels of Steel 36
Whitesnake 5, 28, 38
Wilde, Zakk *2-3*
Wood, Ron 18, *18*

Yardbirds 7, *7*, 10, 18, 27
Yes 8, 28, 31, 34
Young, Angus 21, *21*
Young, George 21
Young, Malcolm 21

Zappa, Frank 34
ZZ Top 39, *40*, 41, 58

Acknowledgments

The publisher would like to thank Adrian Hodgkins the designer, Ron Watson for preparing the index and London Features International for supplying all the photographs. The photographers are as follows:

page 1, Ross Marino, 4 and 5 Kevin Mazur, 8 (right below) Nick Elgar, 9 Ken Regan, 12 (left) Griffin, 12 (right) Neil Preston, 13 (right) Frank Griffin, 14 Nick Elgar, 16 and 17 (top) Michael Putland, 17 (bottom) Ebert Roberts, 18 (below) Govert de Roos, 19 (left) Rik Sins, 19 (right) Phil Loftus, 20 (top, right) George de Sota, 20 (bottom) Kevin Mazur, 21 Ebet Roberts, 23 (top) Geoff Swaine, 24 (top and bottom) RJ Capak, 25 Gene Kirkland, 26 George De Sota, 27 (right) Ross Marino, 28 (top) Paul Cox, 30 and 32 Ross Marino, 33 (top) Steve Rappart, 33 (bottom) Ilpo Musto, 34 Eddie Malluk, 35 Neil Preston, 36 Geoff Swaine, 37 (top) Lynn McAfee, 37 (bottom) Paul Cox, 38 (top) Ebert Roberts, 39 (top and bottom) George de Sota, 40 Colin Mason, 41 (left) Frank Griffin, 41 (right) Ron Wolfson, 42 Ross Marino, 44 Ebert Roberts, 46-7 Kevin Mazur, 48 Govert de Roos, 49 (top) Ross Marino, 49 (bottom) Ilpo Musto, 50 Kevin Mazur, 51 George de Sota, 52 and 53 Ilpo Musto, 54 and 55 George de Sota, 56 Michael Linssen, 57 (top) Nick Elgar, 57 (bottom) George de Sota, 58 Ebert Roberts, 59 (left and right) George de Sota, 60-1 L Felderman, 62 and 63 George de Sota